JEANNE SAUVÉ

Barbara Greenwood

Fitzhenry & Whiteside

Jeanne Sauvé

© Fitzhenry & Whiteside Limited 1989

All rights reserved

No part of this publication may be reproduced in any form without written permission from the publisher.

Fitzhenry & Whiteside
195 Allstate Parkway
Markham, Ontario L3R 4T8

Printed and bound in Canada

Canadian Cataloguing in Publication Data

Greenwood, Barbara, 1940-
  Jeanne Sauvé

(Canadian lives)
ISBN 0-88902-854-0

1. Sauvé, Jeanne, 1922-   — Juvenile literature. 2. Governors general — Canada — Biography — Juvenile literature.* 3. Politicians — Canada — Biography — Juvenile literature. I. Title. II. Series: Canadian lives (Markham, Ont.).

FC626.S38G74 1988   j971.064'092'4
C88-094294-0   F1034.3.S38G74 1988

Editors
Bruce McDougall
Dorothy Salusbury

Designer Darrell McCalla

Picture credits
Children on the Hill Daycare Centre, 36-37
Glenbow-Alberta Institute, 11
Government House, cover, 1, 30-32, 35, 38, 41, 43, 44, 48
Government Photo Centre, 4, 42
John Evans, 44
Metropolitan Toronto Library Board, 22
National Archives of Canada C27281, 28
Prud'homme Historical Committee, 6
Radio-Canada, 24
Reuter, 45
Sauvé family, 7-10, 13-14, 16, 21, 27

Canadian Lives

General Editors
Fred McFadden
Robert Read

Consulting Editors
Doug Dolan
Marjorie E. White

Advisory Panel

Paul Bion	British Columbia
J.G. Bradley	Quebec
Ellen Dunn	Nova Scotia
Jean Hoeft	Alberta
Eric Norman	Newfoundland
Agnes Rolheiser	Saskatchewan
Leslie Steeves	Prince Edward Island
Mary Lou Stirling	New Brunswick
Len Zarry	Manitoba

Titles

Brian Orser	Swimmers
Jeanne Sauvé	Bravery
David Suzuki	Entrepreneurs
Laurie Graham	Kids' Writers
Bryan Adams	Painters
Karen Kain	Musicians
Robert Bateman	Track & Field
Wayne Gretzky	Pioneers

971.064
GRE

1
CHAPTER

Ottawa, May 14, 1984

Canada's New Governor-General

The crowd of school children cheered and waved their red and white Canadian flags. A grey limousine swept past them and up the curved driveway to the Parliament Buildings. As the car stopped in front of the Peace Tower, soldiers in bright red uniforms snapped to attention. A military band played "O Canada."

Jeanne Sauvé stepped out of the car. A small, elegant woman, she started up the steps toward the Prime Minister of Canada. He guided her through the long corridors to the Senate Chamber. There, eleven hundred guests watched as she walked along the red-carpeted aisle to the Senate Throne.

Once she was seated, the Prime Minister began the ceremony that would install Jeanne Sauvé as the twenty-third Governor-General of

PB 92-189/08154

Canada. It was the sixth time a Canadian had been appointed to the highest position in the land and the first time a woman had held the office.

Jeanne Sauvé was a convent-educated girl, born in a tiny town in the middle of the Canadian prairies. Now she had become Her Excellency, the Governor-General, the Head of State, and the Queen's representative in Canada.

It wasn't a smooth or an easy road. But as she once said about herself, "I don't walk all over people to get what I want, but in my own way, I'm a fighter. When I believe in something, I have enormous confidence in myself."

Jeanne Sauvé , the first woman to serve as Governor-General of Canada

CHAPTER 2

Early Life

Prud'homme, Saskatchewan, as it was around the time Charles Benoît and his family moved there. The town's name was Howell until the residents changed it to Prud'homme in 1922. The community thought that the name of their town should be French because most of them were francophones

From the Prairies to Ottawa

Jeanne Benoît was born on April 16, 1922, in Prud'homme, a small French community in Saskatchewan. Although it was only a village with a dozen houses, a general store, a post office and two grain elevators, it had a French convent school attached to the Church of Saints Donatien and Rogatien. That was important to Jeanne's father, Charles Benoît. He wanted his children to attend good schools and learn to speak clear and accurate French.

Charles and his wife, Anna, whose maiden name was Vaillant, had moved their family to the west in the difficult days after the First World War. Jobs were scarce in Ottawa, where Charles had been born and had grown up. Soldiers returning from the First World War competed fiercely for work in the eastern part of Canada.

Baby Jeanne is surrounded by other members of her family at their home in Prud'homme

The West, however, was just opening. Trainloads of Ukrainian and Hungarian immigrants were streaming out to farm the prairies. Many families from eastern Canada were moving west as well. Charles, who was a carpenter and builder, felt that many of the new arrivals would need houses. He would surely be able to provide a good life for his family on Canada's opening frontier.

Charles built a number of houses and other buildings in Prud'homme and nearby communities. By the time Jeanne was three years old, work was harder to find. Charles was also worried about schools. The Benoîts now had six children. Jeanne's older sisters, Berthe and Lina, who were 14 and 12, had already been sent back to Ottawa to finish their schooling. In December 1926, Charles and Anna took the rest of their family, Armand, Annette, Jeanne, and baby Jean, back east.

The train ride from Saskatchewan to Ottawa took three days and four nights. The Benoît grandparents and Grandmother Vaillant met Jeanne and the rest of the family at Union Station in downtown Ottawa. They soon became beloved figures in Jeanne's world.

Once the luggage was unloaded from the train, the family headed off to the Vaillant farm at Ste. Cécile de Masham, 27 kilometres north of Ottawa. For the next few weeks, Charles looked for a house. He wanted to live in a French community close to good separate schools and near a church with many parish activities to interest his growing children. He finally found a house on Carling Avenue in Ottawa. It was the first of several the family lived in as Jeanne grew up.

In July 1926, Jeanne's youngest sister Lucille was born. Jeanne was now the fifth of seven children but she never felt lost in the middle of a large family. Her parents encouraged each child to be an individual. Jeanne felt more like Jean and Lucille's older sister than like a middle child. She always looked after them.

Notre Dame du Rosaire

In September 1927, Jeanne started school at Notre Dame du Rosaire convent. She was taught primarily in French, the language the family spoke at home. "My father and mother did not allow us to speak English at home," she says. "My father always explained: 'This is not because we do not like the English, but because if we do not speak French at home we will not speak it well.' In those days Ottawa was not as French as it is now. We felt very much like a minority."

Jeanne loved everything about school, even her uniform with its long, black stockings

Ottawa, 1930. Jeanne, third from the left, is the fifth of the seven Benoît children

The Benoît girls all attended
the Notre Dame du Rosaire
convent school in Ottawa.
Jeanne is in the second row

and stiff celluloid collars and cuffs that had to be scrubbed each night with soap and water and a toothbrush. She especially loved the days when her teacher pinned a rosette to her black, pleated bodice to show that she had done her work well. When she arrived home, her father would stand her on the table so she could recite her lessons for him. She loved to perform. In fact, all the Benoît children loved writing and performing. So Charles built them a small stage in a large shed behind the kitchen. Here they entertained the neighbourhood with their plays.

Charles had many ways to keep his children happy. Every Saturday he took them to the Ottawa Public Library. When they had chosen all their books, he would take them to the National Museum or the Parliament Buildings. On one trip, he pointed out to Jeanne Agnes MacPhail, the first woman to be elected to the House of Commons.

"One day you might be in Parliament, Jeanne," he commented. Neither of them realized that Jeanne would achieve even more "firsts" than Agnes MacPhail.

Charles Benoît, Jeanne's father, spent a lot of time with all his children. Jeanne and her father shared a special relationship

CHAPTER 3

Growing Up

Work and Play

By the time Jeanne was ten, Canada, like the rest of the world, was suffering from the Great Depression. Hundreds of companies closed their doors, putting thousands of people out of work. Crop failures added to the problem, causing shortages of food. The Benoît family did not suffer extreme hardships. The children never

Many families suffered extreme hardships during the Depression.

went hungry to bed or shoeless to school as many children did in those hard times. Even so, money was not handed out for frivolous pleasures.

"Things were scarce," she says. "We didn't have bicycles. We wore coats our elders had worn. We felt it very much. But everybody felt it. We weren't odd people out. Children of today who don't have these things compare themselves with others who have a great deal, and that's much harder."

The Benoît children made their own fun. Jeanne spent the summers of her early childhood on the farm with Grandmother Vaillant. There she jumped into piles of hay in the big barn and ate picnics along the river.

All the Benoît children helped on the farm. They fed the chickens, gathered eggs and turned the handle of the cream separator. Jeanne's favourite chore was bringing home the cows in the evening.

When they weren't at the farm, Jeanne's mother found things for them to do at home. "When school closed down for the summer, she used to go out and buy us things that we would embroider," Sauvé says. "That's what we were supposed to do in the summer. I still love it."

When school was in session, however, homework came before playtime. Jeanne's mother even placed schoolwork ahead of

Thirteen-year-old Jeanne was head of a patrol of six Girl Guides

household chores. "She would say, 'If you've lots of homework tonight, I'll do the dishes.' To this day, I think it would have taken us only five minutes, but she wanted us to be free to study."

When she finished her studies, Jeanne liked to swim, play tennis, and ride a bicycle in the summer, or ski and go sledding with her friends in the winter.

Jeanne also joined the Girl Guides. The high ideals of the Girl Guide movement appealed to Jeanne's earnest nature. She also enjoyed organizing her patrol of six guides to provide activities for younger children in the parish. Her need to work toward important goals and to organize became important drives in her adult life.

1935-1940: The Teenage Years

Throughout her teenage years, Jeanne excelled at school. She took part in plays and musical performances at St. Jean Baptiste Church and often made speeches.

"I was at school with nuns, and we always had little ceremonies," Sauvé says. "We received the parish priest, the bishop, sometimes the inspector, and I was often chosen to make

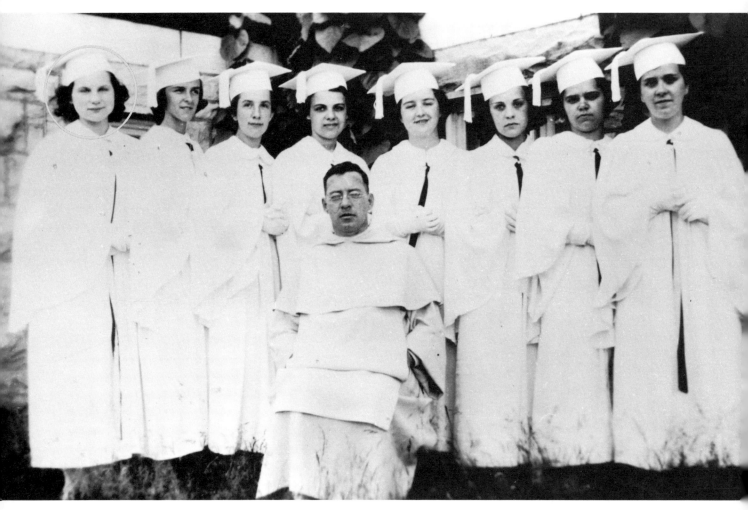

Graduation, 1940, Notre Dame du Rosaire convent. Jeanne wanted to go on to university

the speech of welcome, from the time I was very small."

In her final year of high school, Jeanne faced a problem. She had been educated in French. But her final exams, set by the Province of Ontario, had to be written in English. Her teachers tried to help Jeanne and her classmates. "We always had a French reader and an English reader," she says. But they were far more familiar with French.

Despite her concern, Jeanne passed her exams, in English, with First Class Honours. She also won a scholarship for university. She had wanted to go to university since she started high school.

University, One Way or Another

In 1940, a high school graduate could get a good job without a university degree. Charles still had school fees to pay for his two youngest children, Jean and Lucille. Charles had steady work, but he still did not think he could pay Jeanne's room and board at university. He said she would have to turn down the scholarship and get a job.

Jeanne did not give up so easily. She decided to earn her own room and board during the summer so she could take the scholarship in the fall. But her parents did not approve of their daughter working in the summer. It just wasn't done.

Finally, Jeanne decided to find a full-time job and to take university courses at night. Her determination to find a solution acceptable to all would earn Jeanne more than a university education, as her life progressed.

CHAPTER 4

Looking For Directions

Jeanne and fellow members of the JEC, Montreal. They worked very hard even though the pay was poor

A Time to Question

Jeanne found a job as a translator for the federal Department of National Defence. In the evenings, she attended classes at the University of Ottawa. In her spare time, she participated in local activities. One organization in particular, the Jeunesse étudiante catholique (JEC) or Young Catholic Students, caught her attention.

"It was a Catholic action movement based on the philosophy that as a Catholic, you should be dedicated to improving your environment," she says.

The leaders of the movement taught that young people had the right to question what was happening in the church and in the country. Some church and community leaders disagreed with these ideas. They felt young people should listen to their elders with respect and not challenge them. But Jeanne had many questions

The JEC movement attracted many young people who would later make names for themselves in politics: Pierre Juneau, Chairman of the CRTC, Minister of Finance Marc Lalonde, newspaper editor Claude Ryan, and Pierre Trudeau, Prime Minister of Canada, were among the group Jeanne worked with in those years.

to ask, and the JEC encouraged her to ask them.

Jeanne rose quickly through the organization. As Ottawa president, she learned about leadership. She attended conferences in Montreal and Quebec City. Intelligent and fluently bilingual, she attracted attention from the JEC's head office in Montreal. She was asked to move there to work.

Jeanne had already considered moving to Washington to work for the Canadian government. But her father refused even to allow her to apply for the job. A young girl living alone in a foreign country? Unthinkable!

But Jeanne was restless. She needed a challenge. She liked the idea of working in Montreal, in a completely French community. Two things made her hesitate: she had never lived away from her family before, and the JEC had very little money. Rather than a decent salary, she would receive only a small allowance of seven dollars a week. Her father thought she was throwing away her life. But if she had to leave home, he would rather see her in Montreal than in Washington.

On August 31, 1942, Jeanne telegraphed the good news to her future roommate, Jacqueline Ratte. She would arrive on the 7:10 train. At 20 years old, Jeanne had begun her great adventure.

Montreal: A New Approach

Jeanne and her roommate shared a rent-free room in a converted office building. They had no place to cook. The bathroom was two corridors away. At night, their footsteps echoed through the deserted building. But they didn't mind. They worked so hard and for such long hours that they spent hardly any time in their tiny room.

Jeanne's first assignment was to write articles and give speeches about the work of the JEC. Because she could think clearly and logically, she often spoke without notes and composed articles directly on her typewriter, without making rough drafts. She told her audiences how the JEC worked for political reform, religious enlightenment, and better social services.

"We wanted to improve the school environment," she remembers. "The schools in Quebec were run by nuns and brothers and priests. Some of them thought certain books were not right. We said these books were essential to the widening of our culture. So we forced the establishment of libraries." The JEC also organized trips outside the classroom, so students could view museums. It taught students how to organize politically to change

Canadian New
Draftees Go a

DUPLESSIS SAYS QUEBEC 'HAS BEEN BETRAYED'

Quebec, Nov. 24 (CP)—Premier Duplessis said in a statement here tonight that he hoped the members of Parliament "now discussing this most important ~~pro~~blem (conscription) will not ~~~~ they must act accord- ~~~~ked news-

CONSCRIPTION ONLY ANSWER, SAYS MASSON

Windsor, Nov. 20 (Special)—Lt.-Co George SY. Masson, recently returned civilian life in Windsor, has demanded in mediate conscription be inaugurated b the Federal Government to ensuite "ade quate and properly trained reinforce ments." He made the request in a lette forwarded Hon. Norman A. MeLarty, Sec retary of State.

apers Demand
Reinforcement

QUEBEC LIBERAL CRIES 'TREASON' ON DRAFTEES

By KENNETH C. CRAGG
Ottawa, Nov. 24 (Staff) — A short and bitter attack today against the Government by Wilfred La Croix, Quebec-Montmorency, directly after he left his front-row Liberal seat to take a new place with Quebec Independents in Opposition, immediately before adjournment of the House of Commons, was ordered by Prime Minister King to be expunged from the records of Parliament.

Public controversy arose over Quebec's role in the war

the rules that governed them. It held seminars and published newspapers and training booklets, and took them to colleges throughout Quebec and the rest of Canada.

1939-1943: War and Death

In September 1939, Canada joined Britain in declaring war on Germany. Trainloads of soldiers passed through Montreal on their way to Halifax. There, they would board ships that would take them to Britain. In Quebec, English-speaking young people felt it was their duty to join the armed forces and fight in Europe. But many French-speaking young people felt the war was a British, not a Canadian, problem, and they refused to enlist. Growing up in Ontario had made Jeanne feel differently than other French-speaking youths. "I don't consider the English my enemies," she says. "They are part of us." Her older brother, Armand, was already in the Army, and her youngest brother, Jean, had joined the Air Force.

In 1943, Jeanne crossed the country, lecturing about the JEC. She stopped in Winnipeg, Calgary, Vancouver, and many smaller communities to make speeches to students in

schools, colleges and churches. These trips
exposed her to many people, with different
backgrounds than hers. She realized that Canada
was made up of numerous communities and
cultures, each with its own point of view. She
became impatient with Quebec's narrow
attitude. In later years, this feeling lay at the
heart of her strong sense of nationalism, which
influenced her whole political career.

In 1943, Jeanne also suffered a terrible
shock. Unexpectedly, her father died. But she
was a reserved and private person, and she could
not share her sorrow with anyone outside her
family. In Montreal, she buried her grief by
throwing herself deeply into her work.

Parades and Marriage

Jeanne soon became national president of the
JEC. She worked so hard that she had little time
for a social life. After hours, she sat in
restaurants and cafes, arguing about politics with
other young students, including Maurice Sauvé,
a law student at the University of Montreal.

Maurice was as energetic and clever as
any of the young people Jeanne worked with.
He was also a brilliant organizer.

In 1946, Jeanne was co-ordinating the
JEC's Fifteenth Anniversary Congress.
Twenty-five thousand students from across

20

North America and Europe would attend a pageant, a Mass, and a lunch at a stadium in Montreal. Someone had to organize the parade.

Maurice Sauvé was studying hard to pass his law exams and had to find summer jobs to pay for his next year at school. But he made time for the task. He plotted the parade route carefully through Montreal. He assigned spotters with signs and loudspeakers to control the crowds. The parade went off without a hitch.

Jeanne was impressed, but she still thought of Maurice only as a co-worker. Maurice, however, saw in Jeanne the kind of woman he wanted for a wife: clever, independent, and attractive. But he didn't begin courting her in earnest until he won a scholarship to study at the London School of Economics. He would be spending four years in Europe and he wanted Jeanne at his side.

On September 24, 1948, Jeanne and Maurice were married. They left immediately for Europe. Jeanne's life was about to take another direction.

Jeanne and Maurice left for Europe immediately after getting married

CHAPTER 5

A New Career Begins

London and Paris

Jeanne and Maurice Sauvé arrived in London, England, in 1948. Jeanne was 26 years old. They had little money, so Jeanne found a job as a tutor. Life in England was hard. Food was in short supply, and the government allowed people to buy only limited quantities of meat, butter, sugar, and other scarce items. Despite these difficulties, the Sauvés liked England.

In September 1950, they moved to Paris. Jeanne had been offered a job with the United Nations. Meanwhile, Maurice completed his PhD. Both of them enjoyed living in Paris, the centre of French culture. Jeanne still longed to go to university. She had taken some classes at Ottawa University, but she had not finished her degree. In Paris, she attended the Sorbonne. She received her degree in French Civilization in May 1952.

Later that summer, the Sauvés returned to Canada. "We had to see if we were able to fit in, and continue doing the reforms we believed in," Jeanne Sauvé says. "Also, I think politics was already at the backs of our minds."

A Changed Province

The Sauvés returned to a depressing situation. In their four years abroad, the energy and enthusiasm for social change seemed to have died in Quebec. The government of Premier Maurice Duplessis held the province in a stranglehold. Workers could not join unions to fight for better conditions.

Maurice Sauvé believed passionately in the right of workers to have a voice in the running of their factories. He began working for the organization that would later become the Confederation of National Trade Unions. His first job was to teach textile workers how to negotiate their contracts.

Maurice Duplessis was Premier of Quebec from 1936 to 1959, except for a four-year period during World War II. He and his party, the Union Nationale, worked together with other factions to keep trade unions weak in Quebec

Broadcasting at the CBC

Meanwhile, Jeanne Sauvé considered her strengths: an ability to write, to speak in public, to organize both people and material. She approached the Canadian Broadcasting Corporation for a job, and was hired.

The fifties were an exciting period in broadcasting. Television had just arrived in Canada. Experienced radio broadcasters had to learn to present their material in new ways. Sauvé learned right along with them.

"I was doing radio, but I wanted to go to television," she says. "So I walked into a producer's office." The producer asked Sauvé to devise a program to teach women how to sew little boys' pants. "I bought a pattern and made my own theories on how to teach it," she says. Halfway through the show, the sewing machine jammed. Sauvé lost track of the script, and the show ended in confusion.

Despite that setback, Sauvé worked in television for 20 years. She interviewed everyone from politicians to housewives. In the process, she became well-known on the French and English networks of the CBC. She particularly enjoyed a program called "Opinions," on which she interviewed teenagers about their hopes and concerns.

Sauvé had started the show on the

Jeanne worked for the Canadian Broadcasting Corporation for 20 years, using her talent in writing, public speaking, and organization

English-language network in Ottawa. On each show, she interviewed four teenagers on topics ranging from student discipline and parental authority to teenage sex. A CBC producer, Michael Hind-Smith, recalls that Sauvé was "never too solemn. She always had a twinkle in her eye. She could put nervous teenagers at ease."

The program was so successful that she began a French-language version in Montreal. In the staid and cautious climate of Quebec in the 1950s, the show dealt with controversial topics. It was so successful, Sauvé was soon well-known in Quebec. The show ended in 1963 only because she was tired and needed a new direction.

Making Progress as a Woman

Sauvé also conducted public affairs interviews, but her superiors at the CBC would not let her run her own show. "The producers would give the program to a famous journalist who had no TV talent," she says. But they would ask Sauvé to participate to give the show more life.

Meanwhile, Maurice Sauvé had become a federal politician and a cabinet minister. His political opponents attacked the Sauvés. They suggested that, as the wife of a cabinet minister,

Jeanne Sauvé could not remain neutral as an interviewer on the CBC.

In the press, Sauvé said she had stopped making political comments in public after her husband was elected to Parliament. "However," she said, "there is no reason why I can't continue broadcasting and express opinions on other subjects. After all, a wife is still free to hold an opinion, is she not?"

A New Family

On July 30, 1959, the Sauvés' only son, Jean-François, was born. After spending her working life interpreting the problems of women and children for the public, Sauvé now knew first-hand the problems of a working mother. She rearranged her schedule so that she could do much of her writing at home. She kept the baby in his crib, always in her sight. When she was in the studio, Jean-François went with her.

Producers at the CBC didn't always understand that, for Sauvé, her baby came first. When she turned down a trip across the country to interview some prominent Canadians because she was still nursing Jean-François, one producer said bluntly, "You're crazy."

That attitude toward working mothers was one of the things Sauvé was determined to tackle in the next phase of her career — politics.

Jeanne with her son,
Jean-François, in 1962

27

CHAPTER 6

A Cabinet Minister From Quebec

Politics Becomes a Career

From 1963 to 1968, Sauvé carried on with her broadcasting career and raised her son. But as her husband worked as a Member of Parliament, and later as a cabinet minister, she learned about the life of a politician.

In 1968, Maurice Sauvé decided to resign from politics and begin a career in the business world. That year, a group of people who had worked with Sauvé in the JEC were elected to Parliament. Pierre Trudeau became Prime Minister. Many of his close associates in the Liberal party, such as Jean Lesage and Robert Bourassa, were friends of Sauvé. They wanted her to become part of the new government. In 1968, however, she was too

busy raising her son to consider politics.

In 1972, the federal Liberal party again asked Sauvé to run for office. Now, Jean-François was 13, the family had a housekeeper, and Sauvé was ready for a new challenge. What might she accomplish in this new field? she wondered. As a broadcaster, she had written programs that might have influenced people. As a Member of Parliament, she would be in a better position to carry out her ideas. And as a cabinet minister, she would have real power to make things happen. "Having had a career in public affairs, I found it very easy to switch to politics," she says. "The substance is the same. You're just on the other side of the fence."

Even so, it was a difficult challenge. For one thing, the Province of Quebec had never elected a woman to Parliament. Sauvé campaigned hard. She spoke to small groups in shopping malls, walked up and down streets knocking on doors, shook hands with hundreds of people after church, and drank many cups of coffee at small gatherings. She took particular pains to talk to women. It all paid off. On election night, October 30, 1972, Jeanne Sauvé won by 15 000 votes.

Trudeau and the Liberal party won a majority government in June, 1968

Campaigning during the 1974
election. Jeanne won her seat
in Parliament with a majority
in three elections

The next day, Prime Minister Trudeau
asked her to join his cabinet. This was a
remarkable achievement for Jeanne Sauvé. She
was the only woman Minister. She was the first
woman Minister from Quebec. And she was
only the third woman, after Ellen Fairclough
and Judy LaMarsh, ever to hold a cabinet
position.

Sauvé held many positions in her eight
years as a Member of Parliament: she was
Minister of Science and Technology, Minister of
the Environment, and Minister of Communications. In that last position, she encouraged

Canada to build a place for itself in the space and communications industry.

In 1979, Prime Minister Trudeau called an election. Sauvé won again in her riding, this time by more that 31 000 votes. But the Liberal party lost the election. The Conservatives, under Joe Clark, held office for less than four months. Then the Liberals defeated them. For the third time, Sauvé won her riding. Once again, she expected the Prime Minister to offer her a position in his government. But when she heard his offer, she was appalled. "Oh, no. Not that!" she gasped.

As Minister of Environment, Jeanne met people from all over the world. Here, she is in discussion with Henry Kissinger

CLARA TYNER SCHOOL LIBRARY

7
CHAPTER

Speaker of the House

Jeanne is elected as Speaker of the House

The Offer

The Prime Minister wanted Sauvé to become Speaker of the House. The Speaker controls the House of Commons. When Members become angry or upset, the Speaker acts as a referee. He or she decides what Members of Parliament can and cannot say in the House of Commons. "As the first woman Speaker of the House, you'll never be forgotten," the Prime Minister told Sauvé.

"Who wants to be remembered?" Sauvé wondered. "I just want to do something I like." But could she turn down the chance to show that a woman could fill this role? Before deciding, she took the train from Montreal to Ottawa to consult with other politicians. Finally, she agreed.

Sauvé knew that the Speaker has a lonely job. Because the Speaker is supposed to be neutral, he or she cannot socialize with former colleagues. Also the workload is very heavy.

Sauvé had two months to prepare herself. She had to learn the 116 rules called Standing Orders of the Commons, which govern the way Members act in the House. She also had to learn to recognize every member of the House, and to remember all their names. She resorted to flashcards to help her recognize the 282 faces.

Madam Speaker

When Parliament convened in April 1980, the Clerk of the House of Commons, who had taught her the Rules of Parliament, should have been at her side to answer questions. But two weeks before the opening of Parliament, the Clerk had fallen ill. On the most difficult day of her working life, Sauvé was on her own.

Dressed in the black robes of her new position, Sauvé followed the Sergeant-at-Arms, who was carrying the gold mace, into the House of Commons. As the oak doors swung open, she wondered if she was indeed entering a lion's cage.

The first months were chaotic and exhausting. Sitting in the ornately carved Speaker's Throne with Members of the Government on her right and Opposition Members on her left, Sauvé worked hard to give members of all political parties equal chances to speak. But some Members complained that she never allowed them to speak. Once, seven of them stalked out of the House in protest.

Meanwhile, Sauvé was still learning the Rules of the House. Occasionally, she made mistakes in rulings. Members wanted to be seen on TV by their constituents, so they prepared questions. If Madam Speaker did not allow them to address the cameras, they felt angry and resentful.

The Speaker of the House of Commons controls the House. He or she decides the order in which Members of Parliament speak, and whether they should speak at all.

The Speaker acts as a referee when Members become angry or upset; therefore he or she must be completely familiar with all the rules that govern Parliamentary procedure. Although the Speaker always enters the House as a member of the governing party, he or she must appear neutral. The Speaker is not supposed to take sides on any political issue.

The first woman Speaker of the House of Commons

"It took lots out of me," she says. "I often felt like walking out of the House when they got so turbulent. I even told the Prime Minister I wanted to leave. He took one look at me and said, 'You know you can't leave until you've proved you can do it.' And that was true."

The Bells

In March 1982, Sauvé faced her hardest test as Speaker. The Liberals proposed a bill to which the Conservatives objected. Sauvé ruled that the bill was in order. The Conservatives were incensed. To show their anger, they first moved that the House adjourn, then left the Chamber before the vote was taken. This meant no more business could be done in the House until the motion was voted on.

To make sure every Member knows a vote is to be taken, bells are rung throughout the five buildings on Parliament Hill. At the same time, the officers called the Party Whip are supposed to round up all their Members and usher them back into the Chamber. The Conservative Whip refused to do this. The vote could not be taken, and the bells kept ringing.

They rang for three days and three nights. During that time, either the Speaker or one of her deputies had to remain in the Chair.

Finally, Sauvé stopped all the bells except the one outside the government House Leader's office. That one rang steadily for 15 days while the Speaker searched for a way out of the problem. But after reading all the rulings made by previous Speakers, Sauvé decided that she could do nothing but wait. "What they were doing was legitimate," she says. "They were Members of Parliament, using procedural wrangling to get their point across."

Every morning, Sauvé called both Leaders to ask them how they were going to solve the problem. Finally, on the fifteenth day, they found a compromise and the business of the House started again.

Cost-cutting and Babysitting

Sauvé was having problems outside the Chamber, as well. The second major duty of the Speaker is to direct the everyday running of the five buildings on Parliament Hill. That means supervising a post office, a press, a police force, restaurants, a beauty salon, a barber shop, and offices. Chefs, librarians, carpenters, translators, tour guides, a carillonneur to play the bells in the Peace Tower, a sculptress to repair the stone work — three thousand people work on Parliament Hill.

The first daycare centre on Parliament Hill

The previous Speaker had ordered a review of Parliament Hill's running expenses. When the report appeared on Sauvé's desk, she was outraged. Taxpayers' money was being wasted everywhere. Jobs were being given to friends of Members. Restaurants were losing money serving Parliamentarians cheap lunches. Supplies were bought in expensive small lots instead of economically, in bulk.

Sauvé acted quickly to set her House in order. Cries of outrage were heard as one department after another was swept out and tidied up. Just by raising slightly the price of meals in the House cafeteria and making the customers clear away their own dishes, she saved $150 000 a year.

In April 1982, Sauvé opened the first daycare centre on Parliament Hill. She felt strongly that women who worked in government offices, whether they were Members of the House or office secretaries, needed a safe and convenient place to leave their babies.

"I tried three times to establish a daycare centre when I was a cabinet minister," she says. "I came up against the obstacle of space at first. And the MPs didn't want babies crying in the basement. I had to fight very hard for it."

But, remembering back to the days when she had carried her son right into the studio at the CBC, she persisted. "When children can see their mothers, they feel secure. So do the mothers. It's better for everyone."

She also had a daycare centre built next to a senior citizens' home in her constituency of Ahuntsic in Quebec. "When I was in politics, I'd go into old people's homes," she says. "They were lonely and depressed because they saw only other old people. In Europe, I saw how the grandmothers look after their grandchildren. That's their vocation."

Thanks to this example, Quebec now has a number of daycare centres attached to senior citizens' homes.

A Job Well Done

By the end of 1983, Sauvé had served three-and-a-half years as Speaker. Through hard work and determination, she had won the respect of the House both for the firm hand with which she controlled the Chamber and the efficient way she ran the buildings. But keeping on top of all of the work was exhausting. It was time for a change.

Just before Christmas, the Prime Minister invited her to lunch. She set off for 24 Sussex Drive with high hopes of being named Ambassador to France. Instead, Pierre Trudeau had another surprise in store for her.

Madam Speaker welcomes United States President Ronald Reagan to the House of Commons during his visit to Ottawa in 1981

CHAPTER 8

Her Excellency The Governor-General

The Highest Position in the Land

On December 23, 1983, the Prime Minister announced that Jeanne Sauvé would be the twenty-third Governor-General of Canada. She was the sixth to be Canadian-born and the first woman ever to be appointed.

Soon after the announcement that she would become Governor-General, Sauvé suffered a serious illness. She did not recover for almost five months. Finally, on Monday, May 11, 1984, she was officially given her new position. Eleven hundred witnesses, including the Lieutenant-Governors from each province, judges of the Supreme Court, and Members of

Jeanne Sauvé and her husband, Maurice, on the day she was appointed Governor-General of Canada

Parliament, watched the proceedings in the Senate Chamber on Parliament Hill. Television cameras broadcast the event to the rest of Canada.

In her first speech as Governor-General, Sauvé pointed out to the people of Canada the role she intended to play. "My task, which I take on publicly before you, is to become better acquainted with my countrymen," she said. "Our common task is to promote tolerance, to help each other, and to reject imitations of freedom. We must be united in spirit if we are to go forward in unity. I ask for your support in the days ahead."

The Work of a Governor-General

In her years as Governor-General, Jeanne Sauvé has lived up to the task she set herself. She has travelled across the country constantly.

She started by making official visits to each province as well as to the Yukon and Northwest Territories. She visited Quebec City to help celebrate the 450th anniversary of French explorer Jacques Cartier's voyage to Canada. In the summer of 1986, she toured British Columbia as part of Vancouver's 100th anniversary festivities. In February, 1988, she opened the Winter Olympics in Calgary.

Events like these make the front pages of the newspapers. But the Governor-General also spends many hours making speeches at universities, city halls, and small public functions across the country. Over and over again Sauvé stresses the lesson she learned decades ago on her first trip across Canada to lecture for the JEC. "Despite our varied racial and ethnic origins," she says, "we are Canadians determined to carry on the building of a great nation."

The Governor-General has two official residences — Government House, also known as Rideau Hall, in Ottawa, and at the Citadel in Quebec City. While in residence, the Governor-General has three major duties.

The first is government business such as opening each session of Parliament, and giving royal assent to each bill that is passed by Parliament, thereby making it law. Second is

The investiture ceremony

Rideau Hall, Ottawa — the Governor-General's residence

Madame Sauvé presents seven-year-old Jonathan Carter with the Medal of Bravery

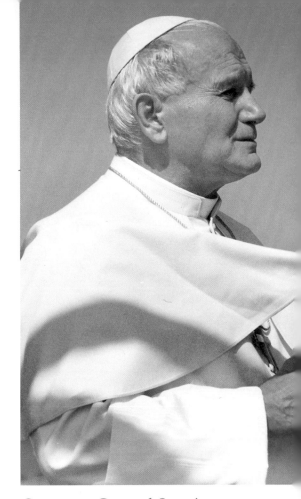

Governor-General Sauvé welcomes His Holiness Pope John Paul II to Canada

presenting several awards including the Order of Canada, to Canadians who have made an outstanding contribution to their country, the Governor-General's Literary Awards, and medals for deeds of heroism.

Finally, the Governor-General is Canada's official host. Important visitors often stay at Rideau Hall. There is a special suite reserved for Her Majesty Queen Elizabeth II. In July 1984, Sauvé gave a reception for His Holiness Pope